Truth and reconciliation commission

By Lord Loveday Ememe and available from Lulu and Amazon

The constitution and policing

Heresy

Starfleet

The supernatural

Creation

Deterrence

Stalking

The media

Adam

Criminal Responsibility

The Wicked

Common Law

Racism

Regulation

Science

Right to Self-determination

ISBN: 978-0-244-49827-6

Table of Content

Demonism

The planet is under red colonization, a political state, made uninhabitable for the natural indigenes of this planet, legal civil beings.

Demonism is the political rule of law or lawlessness, made possible with political role plays or lies, beyond the capabilities of civil legal beings without supernatural powers and senses. Death, illnesses, or diseases including ageing and the corruption of the concept of immortality are important components or spices for demonism to flourish.

The purpose of demonism, in order to establish and maintain lawlessness, is the compromise and the criminalization of civil legal beings, the underestimation of the importance of the civil being in the establishment and maintenance of a civilization.

Demonism is established and maintained by lies. There is a difference between telling the truth officially about the existence of supernatural beings which will require the immediate regulation of supernatural beings and the mandatory fulfilments of their obligations to the state, and telling the truth unofficially informally which maintains the lies and the mad wicked world, leaving the vulnerable at the mercy of the wicked unregulated supernatural beings.

The truth about the existence of supernatural beings pretending to be civil beings without supernatural powers and senses will reveal a lot of crimes or criminal behaviours passed off as naturally occurring requiring the immediate regulation of supernatural beings. Some of these crimes are supernatural phenomena referred to as death, ageing or old age when you are made to look ill or repulsive, illnesses or diseases, poverty, weather problems like flooding, thunderstorms etcetera.

These criminal behaviours make supernatural beings power trip and believe they can plan the lives of the innocent to fit into the demonic culture on earth by misusing their supernatural powers and senses.

In order to maintain demonism, supernatural beings will categorize civil legal beings as medically disabled incompetent beings by lying rather than regulatory disabled competent beings that are rulers as is required by law by telling the truth. The able bodied civil being is disabled compared to the supernatural being for regulatory purposes. The lack of supernatural powers and senses creates the disability.

Article 1 of the European Union charter of fundamental rights, human dignity is inviolable. It must be respected and protected.

Article 1 of the universal declaration of human rights states that all human beings are born free and equal in dignity and rights. They are endowed with reason and conscience and should act towards one another in a spirit of brotherhood. Demonism violates these international laws with its degrading and inhumane treatment of civil legal beings, because demonism flourishes under lies to maintain lawlessness, rather than distinguish civil legal beings as able bodied and different from supernatural beings, they lie about their supernatural constitutions and categorize real civil legal beings as insane. Civil legal beings, human beings, recognized in international law are severely mentally impaired of intelligence for lawlessness social functioning, the political rule of law or demonism because of the lack of supernatural powers and senses. As supernatural beings, beings with supernatural powers and senses are hiding their supernatural constitutions and pretending to be human beings creating hostile demonic living conditions beyond the capabilities of real human beings, they are enabling civil beings to be unlawfully categorized as insane in order to maintain demonism.

Under demonism, illegality and lies are the basis supernatural beings make themselves judges, jury, and executioners of the righteous civil beings contrary to the law. Demonism is established and flourishes when supernatural beings take the place of civil beings as rulers. The use of the wrong standard, the supernatural constitution, is responsible for the creation of discrimination, inequality. It is responsible for the creation of red economics or red capitalism, the market economy, which creates poverty, racism. It is also responsible for the creation of red science, the passing off of the hazardous unscientific as scientific. This is responsible for the terraforming of the planet to create unscientific living conditions, racist hazardous living conditions, for supernatural beings at the expense of the natural indigenes of the planet, civil scientific beings.

Demonism portrays civil scientific beings as under achievers, parasites, weak sickly beings that can only survive on the charity of supernatural beings.

The disability equality rights of civil scientific beings, which are the rights and privileges of a ruler, are undermined under demonism. These disability equality rights of civil beings are either more or less significant depending on the level of technological and scientific advancements in a civilization. The rule of law creates conditions to live and let live, a level playing field that eliminates discrimination that are compromised by demonism.

The unusual interest in civil scientific beings by supernatural beings that results in disruption or obstruction of the lives of civil beings including spells that changes the physiques of civil beings to the ridiculous are demonism in operation. The primary objective of demonism is the persecution and destruction of civil noble beings.

Demonism is the supremacy of the supernatural constitution over civil scientific beings responsible for lawlessness. Under demonism, the hostile wicked nature of the supernatural constitution determines lifestyles and lifespan, the introduction of supernatural phenomena referred to as ageing, illnesses or diseases, and death. Death and resurrection do not have the same effect on supernatural beings as they do on civil beings. Resurrection can be a cure for the supernatural phenomenon death as a healthcare provision but it is not how it is used under demonism. It is used to demonstrate fearlessness by supernatural beings, they are not afraid to die therefore put themselves through the process over and over again.

Demonism is rebellion against an established order; it is lawlessness.

The objective of demonism is to corrupt supernatural beings by feeding their power tripping egos to be worshipped by civil legal beings, which is the case in most cultures around the world. This is the case even when it would mean being slaves or subservient to the supernatural beings that are reds. This is what makes red colonization of the planet possible. Once you accept the criminal way of life you become subservient or subject to the rules of the larger criminal faction, the reds.

Under demonism, supernatural beings are not allowed relationships or associations or contacts with the righteous civil legal beings and can only establish relationships or associations or contacts illegally. Under demonism, supernatural beings lack the discipline or self-control to establish relationships or associations or contacts with righteous civil legal beings legally. For supernatural beings to establish legal relationships or associations or contacts with righteous civil legal beings, will require the self-control or discipline to reject demonism or racism by submitting to righteous civil legal beings as the rulers of the planet, which is the first step in the establishment of the rule of law.

When civil beings experience unusual problems as if unlucky or being picked on, they are as a consequence of demonism. The supernatural constitution is naturally aggressive compared to the standard civil scientific constitution; the purpose of the law is to regulate the supernatural constitution encouraging self-control or discipline. Demonism on the other hand wants the already aggressive supernatural constitution out of control by creating hostile living conditions. Hostile living conditions, encouraging aggression from an already aggressive supernatural constitution threatens the peace and security of civil legal beings. Establishing contact or communication with civil scientific beings supernaturally rather than the legal scientific method are acts of aggression, unlawful under international law. The unlawful supernatural method will most definitely include the invasion of privacy, which includes the further discomfort of the vulnerable, the invasion of the private thoughts of the vulnerable contrary to international law. The legal scientific method for contact and communication with civil scientific beings will require the identification and distinction of civil beings as rulers with rights and privileges and protocols for the necessary checks and balances given the differences between the civil and supernatural constitutions. Demonism is a deviation from the established order created in the garden of Eden by the creator, a supernatural being, and the created, Lord Adam, a civil being, resulting in the unlawful persecution of civil beings. This deviation can be found in all religions, political governments, etcetera that directly, or indirectly advocate the supremacy of supernatural beings over civil beings responsible for lawlessness and the unlawful persecution of civil beings. The rights and privileges of rulers are regulatory disability rights, making any delay in distinguishing civil from supernatural beings as required by law, demonic.

The legal scientific methods for communication or contact or interaction with civil beings are regulatory disability rights for security and insurance that the entitlements, regulatory rights, and privileges of civil beings are not undermined by unlawful unscientific supernatural demonic methods.

The vulnerable are held hostage or are slaves to the supernatural political self-destructive role plays of supernatural beings under the political rule of law that the vulnerable civil beings are exempt from, spells and bullying are used to force their demonic racist way of life on the vulnerable civil being.

Under demonism the victimization of civil beings is a way of life like the game monkey in the middle, where civil beings are the monkeys or the monkey, serious life issues of civil beings are tossed about by supernatural beings as games at the expense of the physical and mental wellbeing of civil beings. The fake assistance for civil beings from attacks from other supernatural beings is designed to make civil beings monkeys in the middle. The method of assistance and the solution under demonism are hostile, degrading, in most cases will prove to be more of a problem than the problem. Civil beings are plagued with demons and corrupt supernatural beings looking for faults, anything to make an issue of, especially when they and their way of life have been rejected, they make rules for civil beings within illegality ensuring that civil beings are always caught in their traps, making the good appear guilty; attack is the best form of defence. Illegal punishments of civil beings make them appear morally superior. These punishments are done without the due process of law because the evidence of wrongdoings on those that are not criminally responsible will not withstand proper scrutiny. These punishments and rules within illegality for civil beings are off the record, they are done supernaturally.

Reds or demons will collect enmity from the jaws of friendship, as a consequence of their hostile attitudes toward civil beings that represent friendship or order. Demons give with one hand and take with the order, show no substance. The reds are responsible for the misapplication of the Christian teachings in the form of the church, the misapplication of governance through democracy or politics, red economics, red science, etcetera, all hostile to the establishment of the real rule of law and civil beings.

The reds want to be seen as the better of two or more evils within an evil system they are responsible for, in order to practice demonism or the persecution of civil beings freely. Red colonization of the planet corrupts other supernatural beings to undermine the establishment of the real rule of law which ensures the constant persecution of civil beings.

Common law which includes the bible, international and domestic legislations only recognize civil beings and protect civil beings from contact or interaction with supernatural beings by prohibiting such contact or interaction. The laws will not permit contact or interaction with civil beings until civil beings have been properly identified and distinguished from supernatural beings as rulers, with all the rights and privileges of rulers.

The racism of demonism ensures that information is provided in a way that only supernatural beings will understand it. This includes red science, although civil beings have been deliberately compromised to be enslaved to red science only supernatural beings will be privy to information on how to get out of the problems of red science. Red science includes supernatural phenomena they refer to as illnesses or diseases. If you do not know how to avoid the problems associated with red science they torture you for not knowing, for not being supernatural.

Given the extremely hostile attitudes of supernatural beings toward civil beings under demonism, should supernatural beings plan the lives of civil beings including the appearance or physique of the civil constitution? The laws, international and domestic legislations, common law which includes the bible say no.

The civil scientific being is the natural constitution of a ruler, and it is not easy being a civil being especially when surrounded by supernatural beings. This sacred natural ability is undermined under demonism and categorized as a medical disorder. Supernatural beings play the role of rulers under demonism by trying to aspire to the qualities of real rulers in order to distinguish themselves from their peers, and pay themselves hundreds of thousands of pounds yearly as rulers.

The eating habits of the majority of the world's population

reflect lawlessness or demonism, the bible confirms that man is vegetarian. The vegetarian society is a charity organization set up to guide the legal person on what is or is not edible. They state that eggs and dairy products are edible. Supernatural beings could have always intended for cow milk and chicken eggs to be edible, their methods of production involve cruelty to animals. This suggests that the methods of production are red. Given what is really possible the production of these products could be legal.

Apartheid

Apartheid is a by-product of demonism or racism, where hostile living conditions are created to meet the needs of supernatural beings at the expense of the physical and mental wellbeing of the natural indigenes of the planet, the civil legal beings. Demonism advocates to live and let die rather than to live and let live, in favour of supernatural beings.

Apartheid is the enforcement of the separation of civil and supernatural beings by rejecting civil beings as rulers and the encouragement of barbaric behaviours from supernatural beings making socialization with supernatural beings impossible because of the delicate nature of the civil scientific being. The barbaric socialization currently practised is beyond the capabilities of the civil scientific being. Lawlessness creates apartheid, which is the alienation and persecution of civil scientific beings without supernatural powers and senses.

During the apartheid created by lawlessness, supernatural beings create the impression of living better lives than civil scientific beings, with the result that civil beings are seen as underachievers. The political objective is to undermine civil scientific beings at the same time undermining the rule of law represented by civil scientific beings.

Life for civil scientific beings become similar to always trying to navigate minefields, under demonism. Every action, interaction, communication etcetera, are misconstrued deliberately by supernatural beings, demons and corrupt supernatural beings, as if civil beings are selling their souls to the devil, willing participants in demonism. This is laughable because civil beings have been deliberately created to be righteous, constituted deliberately to be incapable of lawlessness. Civil beings are representations of god and not supernatural beings as is commonly believed under demonism. This makes socialization with supernatural beings impossible, constructive apartheid.

Any type of interaction or communication or contact, directly or indirectly, with a supernatural being or supernatural beings are misconstrued as authorization or permission to misuse their supernatural powers and senses to torture civil beings contrary to international law.

Only a part of the supernatural constitution is regulated, the part that appears human, the supernatural part of their constitution is not regulated, allowed to bully or intimidate the vulnerable civil being unchallenged or unregulated. The only way to avoid bullying or oppression is to avoid any type of socialization or interaction with supernatural beings. Constructive apartheid is a legal principle, the discrimination against the vulnerable, who because of circumstances beyond their control, refuse to socialize or interact with the wicked. An example of this type of discrimination is when the supernatural powers of supernatural beings are misused to alter the physical appearance of the vulnerable including alterations of the sexual organs, given the obligations of supernatural beings to provide appropriate healthcare to counteract such attacks, relationships or associations or socialization with supernatural beings are impossible because of their complicity in such attacks.

The civil noble being can only interact or socialize in the noble being's official capacity as ruler for the necessary checks and balances given the differences between the civil and supernatural constitutions. This helps eliminate social problems like bullying generated by inequality. The undermining of this sacred determination creates different types of apartheid. The relationships or associations forced on civil beings by supernatural beings where civil beings are not fully themselves because of the failure to distinguish between the civil and supernatural constitutions are types of apartheid.

When you choose to be on your own because of the wickedness of supernatural beings they resort to establishing relationships with civil beings supernaturally against their wills. This type of invasion creates its own type of apartheid. This unwanted interest or invasion, similar to Germany's invasion of Poland during the Second World War or Iraq's invasion of Kuwait in the early nineteen nineties, comes with the oppressor's rules. They use their supernatural powers and senses to make life impossible for you when you are meant to be on your own. Your thoughts are monitored, if you have natural thoughts of repulsion because of oppression they put spells on you to make you feel ill or alter your physique as punishments. When you start to think unnaturally because of oppression, it is a type of apartheid. Given the differences between the civil and supernatural beings, the civil being is no threat to justify this type of monitoring.

Supernatural phenomena referred to as sexually transmitted diseases or illnesses only obstruct civil beings from establishing companionships, making companionship a minefield, uncomfortable, creating another type of apartheid, sexual apartheid.

Evidence suggests that the relationship between the civil and supernatural constitutions will never get better because of the natural retardation of the supernatural constitution, no moral centre, or soul, but the protection of the civil constitution can be improved if the law is applied correctly. These suggest that the pastime of supernatural beings is to make the lives of civil beings miserable, civil beings have barely enough for life's basic needs as if being kept alive to be toyed with by supernatural beings.

Supernatural political role plays under the political rule of law or demonism confirm that supernatural beings have no value for life, including human life, they have no self-respect or dignity, and self-harm and harm others for purposes of demonstrations or attempts to inform rather than the simple direct safe way of communicating. They are willing to threaten the lives and health of the vulnerable including civil beings for this method of communication or this method of regulation within lawlessness. These red methods cater to the hyperactive constitutions of supernatural beings at the expense of law and order, creating additional problems rather than resolutions.

Supernatural beings make the reasonable efforts of civil

beings applied to projects or tasks go to waste because of their superhuman strengths and hyperactive constitutions. They like to create tasks for themselves unnecessarily to cater to their super constitutions, what should be considered serious life issues by the reasonable are treated like jokes and games to play. The effects of efforts on a task are different for the civil and supernatural constitutions, yet supernatural beings make the efforts on a task go to waste requiring the unnecessary repetition of a task or project. This is why none of the laws on this planet gives supernatural beings any authority over civil beings, the laws give civil beings authority over supernatural beings in order to protect civil beings from the supernatural constitution's super hyperactive appetite. Supernatural beings resort to bullying and deceit to give themselves equality by unlawfully pretending to be civil beings within the laws of the planet and make real civil beings vulnerable to super hyperactivity. From the beginning to the end of the bible supernatural beings identified as the wicked have been condemned for their refusal to establish the real rule of law. Civil beings have been distinguished as the meek, the righteous, who will not suffer the same fate as the wicked.

There is the insane practice amongst supernatural beings with civil beings trapped in the middle, red supernatural beings try to be blue and blue supernatural beings try to be red within the demonic system of red colonization. This attempt by blue supernatural beings creates a political faction that is toxic to civil beings. This confirms that regardless of the skin colours of supernatural beings unless they behave lawfully they represent an unacceptable threat to the security of civil beings and the security of the planet. The significance of this determination is that blue supernatural beings believe wrongly that they have an automatic right of access to civil beings although their behaviours are unlawful, criminal. The law clearly requires all supernatural beings to behave lawfully regardless of skin colour especially when in contact with civil beings because of the effects of lawlessness on the delicate constitutions of civil beings.

There is nothing worse than being a demon, whose primary objective is the compromise and criminalization of civil noble beings in order to maintain or create lawlessness, which is the supremacy of supernatural beings over other beings on the planet.

Truth and reconciliation

When relationships, organizations or associations, especially a state are built on lies, they will fail, not work, like a house built on a foundation of quicksand. After the failures, they, most of the time cannot be rebuilt, because of the damage done.

The right to life of civil beings is based on the truth of what is possible and not the lies of demonism.

The truth is that, measured against the civil scientific being, who the planet is meant for, supernatural beings because of their unscientific constitutions are retarded, and their supernatural powers and senses make them dangerous to themselves and those around them. They are not allowed to make decisions for themselves. The peace of supernatural beings or their perceptions of danger are different from civil scientific beings who the planet is meant for, as the natural indigenes of the planet. Supernatural beings are required to let civil scientific beings or the needs of civil scientific beings guide them or their decisions. The direct or indirect judgements of supernatural beings on civil scientific beings are forbidden, treasonous.

The laws including the bible under common law forbid relationships or associations with supernatural beings for the protection of civil beings from the misuse of supernatural powers and senses. The necessary safeguards need to be in place, the distinction of civil beings as rulers with the civil rights and civil privileges, for the necessary checks and balances given the massive differences between the civil and supernatural constitutions. Informality between the two constitutions will inevitably lead to the bullying or oppression or domination of civil beings by supernatural beings. Hell hath no fury like a supernatural being scorned. Normal banter amongst friends could have torturous repercussions for civil beings because of the massive differences in constitutions.

The truth is that companionship is a civil right, which is denied civil righteous beings, in more ways than one, under demonism. This civil right violation is a type of apartheid. The lies of demonism categorize civil righteous beings as clinically or medically insane, creating demonism; they then proceed to misuse their supernatural powers and senses to put spells on civil righteous beings to create the impression of insanity.

The truth is the only way to establish a legitimate state or association or relationship through the real rule of law that takes into account the existence of the civil and supernatural constitutions. A regulatory body or institution has to be legitimate to have the legitimacy to regulate. Legitimacy can only be achieved through the truth.

The truth is not achieved by withholding information or misinformation because it is expected that supernatural beings with their supernatural powers and senses should know the truth anyway, in order to meet the criterion for truthfulness information should be provided as if the information is not already known, as if the recipient is of the civil constitution as the standard.

The truth is that international laws that protect the legal

person, especially the universal declaration of human rights have already instructed that the real rule of law should be established. The deliberate hijack or sabotage by supernatural beings pretending unlawfully to be legal persons of the determination made by international law is the reason for demonism or lawlessness. Some of these determinations made in the universal declaration of human rights can be found in article 1, which states that all human beings are born free and equal in dignity and rights. They are endowed with reason and conscience and should act towards one another in a spirit of brotherhood. These determinations can also be found in article 3, which states that everyone has the right to life, liberty, and security of person. The main threat to the security of the legal person including the threat to the legal person's right to self-determination is the supernatural constitution. This will suggest that the establishment of a police service to regulate the supernatural constitution to keep the peace of the civil legal person is of paramount importance.

The truth is that common law requires supernatural beings, the working class, uncivilized beings, to have a basic education of how to behave around the nobility, civil legal being, or beings. This is in order not to be offensive, in reality, not to give offence because of the differences between the civil and supernatural constitutions, to safeguard the mental and physical wellbeing of the civil noble constitution.

Unfortunately, to further their demonic objectives or

bugging, supernatural beings use jokes and games to try to create unauthorized or unlawful access to their victims, civil legal beings. They also use relationships or associations or contacts or communications with theirs victims to abuse mentally and physically. They also use the interests of their victims to harm them, for example, food, cigarettes, companionships, etcetera.

The problem with being judge, jury and executioner under demonism like the reds is that when they are not fit to have contact or to communicate or to associate with civil beings and they deem themselves fit to, civil beings cannot complain, similar to a Jew under Nazism making a complaint to a Nazi about another Nazi, no checks and balances. Under demonism, the time of civil righteous beings is of no value to supernatural beings, and there is no consideration that the time of the civil being could be valuable to the civil being. Spells of deception or lies are cast on civil beings for long periods with no regard for how that might affect the personal development of the civil being. Spells of incapacitation they refer to as illnesses or diseases are cast on civil beings contrary to common law with no regard for the long- term psychological effects, or the value of the time or period of incapacitation to the civil being.

Supernatural beings try to hide behind supernatural political role play, which is another way of referring to demonism or lies, to try to assassinate civil legal beings or to compromise the physical and mental wellbeing of civil beings with supernatural phenomena they refer to as illnesses or diseases. They also hide behind lies to damage the properties of civil beings with supernatural phenomena they refer to as natural disasters or the acts of god. These disguised supernatural attacks on civil beings are contrary to common law and contrary to international law, in particular, article 3 of the universal declaration of human rights, the right to life. The truth is that work for the purposes of remuneration and regulation or government is defined discriminatorily to give unfair advantages to supernatural beings under demonism, which does not take into account that civil beings work naturally as civil beings, contrary to common law and contrary to articles 7,21,23 of the universal declaration of human rights.

Unfortunately, unregulated relationships or associations or communications or contacts or interactions with civil beings, when supernatural beings refuse to tell the truth about their supernatural constitutions and are unsupervised by the law, are different types of paedophilia.

The truth is that for the real rule of law to be established supernatural beings have to be identified as what they are, and not as what they are not. They should not be regulated as what they appear to be but as what they are, because appearances can be deceptive.

Demonism is fed by lies, and the nature of the supernatural constitution will suggest that supernatural beings are working collectively to establish and maintain demonism regardless of their skin colours.

The concept of immortality has been corrupted to fit into the barbarism of demonism, rather than the good stay young, their idea of good, die young and go to their idea of heaven or warrior's paradise. The truth is that because of the nature of the supernatural constitution, death, illnesses or diseases, ageing, are directly or indirectly voluntary for supernatural beings regardless of appearances. The nature of the civil constitution means that these supernatural phenomena, death, illnesses or diseases, ageing, are forced on civil beings contrary to common law because civil beings are incapable of consenting.

The truth is not hostile but is comforting. The truth is hostile only to the criminally minded.

The truth is that what makes the differences in skin colours more pronounced amongst supernatural beings is lawlessness or demonism, the establishment of the real rule of law makes the differences redundant.

The truth is that the right to life of the legal person is not in degrees or political but is absolute or legal. This also applies to defences against supernatural phenomena referred to as illnesses or diseases, which should not include torture in the provision of such defences. This determination is derived from the reality of what is possible and not the unreality of the political role plays associated with lawlessness.

Ageing(looking old), diseases or illnesses, death etcetera whether as punishments or not are directly or indirectly voluntary for supernatural beings, they have the choice to opt out, the laws for purposes of equality require the same choice be given to civil beings without altering their civil states or constitutions.

The state should have adequate defences against the outbreak of lawlessness, which include deterrents from supernatural attacks, when the defences are unlawfully breached there should be adequate healthcare provisions that can counteract any supernatural attack referred to as illness or disease. For the healthcare provision or system to be lawful it must incorporate all the civil rights of the legal person who is the primary beneficiary of the system. The main civil rights that must be incorporated into the healthcare system are the civil right to life and the civil right to be free from torture. Unfortunately, the current healthcare system given the reality of possibility is inhumane, and born out of red demonic science, unscientific. This was reemphasized in common law through Jesus Christ in the bible, who healed the sick and raised the dead immediately as soon as he became aware of the problem. Unfortunately, under demonism supernatural beings are waiting to be worshipped by civil beings in more ways than one, first. You need to note that Jesus Christ in the bible was a representation of supernatural beings and the recipients of the healthcare were representations of civil beings. Healthcare provisions for the civil being have been determined to be unconditional because common law made the determination that the civil being is not criminally responsible given the differences between the civil and supernatural constitutions. This remains the case whether or not supernatural beings like or dislike the actions or behaviour of the civil being.

Supernatural beings that hide their supernatural identities and neglect their obligations to the state are criminals. Supernatural beings that also reveal their supernatural identities in an unlawful way are behaving criminally or unlawfully. Supernatural beings have to be identified and registered as what they are in a lawful way, and learn as supernatural beings how to behave or interact lawfully. Unfortunately, when supernatural beings reveal themselves to civil beings in an unlawful way especially by putting themselves in the way or disrupting a scientific process, they are regarded by common law as spells cast on civil beings. Some African cultures have some healthcare provisions in place for the legal person, in the form of native doctors to serve as remedies and protections from supernatural attacks. Although, these healthcare provisions can be improved and delivered truthfully, and not allowed to be tainted with the lies of political role plays.

One of the first references to the criminal law principle, criminal responsibility, after this was first implied about the civil being, not being criminally responsible, in the garden of Eden in the relationship between the creator and Lord Adam, was in Luke 23:34 when Jesus Christ who was a representation of the supernatural constitution said about the people gathered, who were representations of the civil constitution, during his crucifixion, father forgive them for they know not what they do.

Implied in the relationship between the creator and Lord

Adam, the civil being was never meant to know about ageing or looking old, illnesses or diseases and death. These were meant to be used as types of punishments for the criminally responsible supernatural beings.

These supernatural phenomena referred to as illnesses or diseases including ageing or looking old are lies based on the nonexistence of supernatural beings introduced under demonism as natural occurrences that man has no solutions to prevent. It should be noted that for the purposes of solutions to these unscientific supernatural phenomena, supernatural beings are referred to as man, which is a lie. They are referred to as man which is a lie, as a consequence neglecting their duties under common law. The unscientific red procedures or processes used to ascertain whether or not you have contracted one of their red supernatural phenomena referred to as illnesses or diseases are torturous for civil legal beings but not for supernatural beings. This confirms that the current healthcare system is racist deliberately unlawfully persecutory to the meek civil being. Unfortunately, supernatural beings use lies under demonism or lawlessness to satisfy the violent urges associated with the supernatural constitution, urges that should be brought under control with the real rule of law. These violent urges are responsible for the organized crime or organized fighting disguised as a civilization, a political state. These lies assist supernatural beings to kill or commit murders, and are responsible for the planet earth to suffer the supernatural phenomena referred to as natural disasters, plane crashes, motor accidents, etcetera.

As a consequence of the self-destructive nature of the supernatural being, the law even under demonism protects the vulnerable civil being; the same way in the fictional film merchant of Venice the law protected the vulnerable Antonio from the wicked Shylock. This is achieved by the law only recognising the civil being, protecting the civil being from the self-destructive role plays of supernatural beings, although supernatural beings try to undermine or ignore these legal technicalities found in international and domestic legislations.

The establishment of a legal state, Earth

It is through the guaranteed civil rights of the civil legal being that a civilization is created and supernatural beings are protected from their peers.

The civil state or constitution of man is the foundation of a civilization. The wellbeing of the delicate civil being is essential to the establishment and maintenance of a civilization.

Given my experiences as a civil being surrounded by supernatural beings, are supernatural beings ready for civilization? The answer to that is no. They do not appear to understand the concept, its connection to civil beings. This is quite evident in the United Nations that uses the needs of supernatural beings as the basis for a civilization, ending up with the creation of a political state rather than a legal state, always at war with itself.

The nature of the supernatural constitution will suggest that the military with its discipline and level of force is the appropriate method to police supernatural beings to keep the peace, a type of martial law or police state.

The peace of civil beings has universal application, making civil beings law lords or commissioners of police.

Common law will confirm that the military was born from the nobility, and the nobility is modelled on civil beings.

Common law confirms that the planet earth was meant for civil beings as its indigenes. Since the civil state or constitution is the law in living form, earth was always meant to be a peaceful planet, paradise.

Supernatural beings make references to the names used to

identify the civil state or constitution, like, law lord, president, monarch, commissioner, etcetera, politically to impersonate civil beings blasphemously, responsible for the planet to be at war with itself. Common law, the bible, makes the determination that the name of the lord should not be used in vain as supernatural beings currently do under the political lawless system.

Unfortunately, supernatural beings because of their hyperactive constitutions like to create living conditions with a lot of problems, challenges, or obstacles to overcome, a warrior's paradise on planet earth. These conditions are racist because they are extremely hostile to beings that are not supernatural beings like civil beings the natural indigenes of planet earth.

Supernatural racist living conditions make the lives of civil beings hell unlawfully, and as a consequence common law made the determination that the condemnation to hell of the wicked to be proportionate to the crimes against civil beings. The effects of their crimes against civil beings were deemed proportionate to their condemnation to hell given the differences between the civil and supernatural constitutions. Supernatural beings either want to tell the truth to facilitate the establishment of the rule of law, the creation of a legal state, or maintain the lies and remain enemies of the state, unlawful persecutors of civil beings.

What divides the different political factions, the political state and freedom fighters, political religions, political cultures, or political countries within the political state, etcetera are based on lies to cater to the hostile nature of the supernatural constitution at the expense of the physical and mental wellbeing of the vulnerable including the wellbeing of the natural indigenes of the planet earth, the civil legal beings.

Unfortunately, freedom fighters around the world are not fighting for the establishment of the real rule of law but are fighting for political variations of the political rule of law. They want to graduate from the oppressed to become the oppressors.

The establishment of the state, an extension of the civil scientific being, bridging the gap between the civil and supernatural constitutions through science and technology, also serve to regulate supernatural beings. Supernatural beings for purposes of law and order are then required to use the alternatives of science and technology rather than the disruptive, disorderly supernatural powers and senses. The objective is to keep the peace. The peace of the civil legal state is universal while the peace of the supernatural political state is not universal.

The United Nations an organization meant to facilitate the establishment of a legal state has been constructed with the foundation of lies undermining the sacredness of the civil being. This has led to the creation of a political state because the organization which should have been used as a commission for the establishment of a legal state has been hijacked by the reds for red colonization of planet earth.

Author's notes

My book truth and reconciliation commission identifies the real causes of lawlessness responsible for an insane world, and the reluctance of what are meant to be law enforcement agencies to establish and maintain law and order.

Red or demonic colonization of the planet is an act of aggression against civil legal beings, crimes against humanity, and genocide or attempted genocide.

Civil beings have guaranteed civil rights that are constantly being undermined by demonism contrary to common law. Common law identifies the beginning of the protection of animals, or animal rights, when Noah was instructed to build a ship in order to save humans and animals from the flooding. This suggests that animals do have the right to life and should not be eaten by humans and other animals. These rights are being undermined by the insanity of demonism.

I am of African origin, the Ibo tribe in Nigeria. The Ibo language's word for tradition is omenala, which is a reference to the civil state.

The lies of supernatural beings collectively regardless of skin colour are responsible for lawlessness, poverty, discrimination or inequality, organized crime or organized fighting. Supernatural beings appear to like hostile living conditions, which are hostile to the delicate nature of the natural indigenes of the planet, civil legal beings.

These lies are responsible for the failure of the United Nations commission to establish a legal state.

The civil being is naturally law abiding while the supernatural being is not naturally law abiding but has to behave appropriately to be law abiding given the differences between the civil and supernatural constitutions. This suggests that when supernatural beings accuse the civil being of wrongdoing or criminal behaviour, they are either operating under demonism or they do not understand the concept or mechanism of the law, how it operates or is applied in practice.

Under demonism, the red colonization of the planet, supernatural beings collectively put in place different types of thorns in the different geopolitical zones for the vulnerable civil beings. This will suggest that they never intended to have genuinely good relationships with civil legal beings.

It is terrible that civil beings under demonism, rather than live life, are reduced to living like slaves used for sport by supernatural beings, their times are wasted recovering from one mental or physical abuse after another. This is the case although the laws including common law the bible exempt and protect civil beings from the self-destructive supernatural political role plays.

Supernatural beings speak the same language metaphorically; they behave the same way responsible for lawlessness around the world, red colonization of the planet. The way to achieve individual rights and individuality, to make supernatural beings to speak different languages, metaphorically, a type of separation, is through the establishment of the real rule of law.

The United Nations commission must incorporate the truth

and reconciliation into its primary objective to establish a legal state, the rule of law.

Direct and indirect aggression linked to the aggressive excesses of the supernatural being when compared to the legal scientific civil being must be regulated for the establishment of peace and security. This is why what are considered aggressive practices or actions like what you eat, methods of communication, methods of establishing relationships etcetera must be legal or stopped if considered aggressive or illegal.

Under demonism, supernatural beings misinterpret or misapply their obligations to civil beings as rulers, as if having dominion or authority over civil beings contrary to the law. It is important to note that the concept of science has always been misapplied by supernatural beings responsible for lawlessness, chicken eggs and cow milk if intended to be edible can be produced independent of chicken and cows given what is possible, making their production legal.

Demonism creates conditions unlawfully for supernatural beings to play gods with the needs of the vulnerable, converting the mandatory legal rights of civil beings to political rights. This has the horrific effect of converting the vulnerable civil beings from rulers to slaves.

Demonism creates conditions for supernatural beings to power trip with the lives of the vulnerable.

The civil legal being works naturally by remaining a civil being, which attracts the peace or living conditions for the civil being that has universal application. It is not easy to be a civil being especially surrounded by supernatural beings. This natural sacred self-sacrifice is wasted by demonism and weaponized to harm the civil being. The vulnerable nature of the civil being compared to the supernatural being is used to torture the civil being constantly mentally and physically by demons and corrupt supernatural being.

The natural assurances or security, the supernatural excesses of the supernatural constitution provide for the supernatural being are provided for the civil legal being in a different way. They are provided for the civil being as an independent being, as ruler, for regulatory purposes through a legal state. This equality of security can only be achieved by legal methods and for legal purposes. Security includes the right to life, adequate healthcare system, freedom from poverty, access to information, etcetera, whether or not supernatural beings give theirs up because of stupid barbaric practices. It should not affect the civil being's right to these provisions. As a consequence of the red colonization of the planet, and the resulting red world economy means that all monies or currencies are directly or indirectly tainted with cruelty to animals and the persecution of civil legal beings.

Unfortunately, because of the way supernatural beings are constituted they undermine state security or treat the concept of state security as jokes and games, undermining the security of the vulnerable which includes civil beings. Supernatural beings undermine the state security concept which includes an adequate healthcare system because they see themselves as invincible, there are circumstances that a supernatural being or supernatural beings could be so incapacitated or threatened by their peers that they will require the intervention of an adequate state security service which includes a healthcare system.

For purposes of law and order, equality, the fair distribution of wealth or resources, goods and services must be provided through the state given the existence of both civil and supernatural beings.

The king of kings or the lord of lords is another way of referring to the law or laws that supersedes other laws. Like international or universal law. As I explained in previous books, the civil being without supernatural powers and senses is the law in living form.

The civil being, without supernatural powers and senses, works naturally by being and remaining civil without the need for activity or activities to confirm that the civil being is working, unlike the supernatural being. This creates problems for the civil being because of the bullying nature of the supernatural being who insists on applying the work standard meant for the supernatural being on the civil being. The bullying effects of demonism undermine the sacred work of the civil being.

Unfortunately, the propaganda of demonism categorizes masculinity with the supernatural and categorizes femininity with the civil. Given that males and females are supernatural, with supernatural powers and senses, the civility of the civil being is being mocked or undermined. The civil being is the alpha male because masculinity is linked to the civil and not the supernatural.

As a consequence of the racist demonic interpretation of masculinity, racist supernatural beings put themselves in positions meant for civil beings as if being protective of or helpful to civil beings.

Lies are used by demons and corrupt supernatural beings to make the afterlife, an extension of demonism, appear attractive to civil beings.

The caste system when applied correctly achieves equality while establishing the real rule of law. The caste system is the distinction of the civil noble constitution from the supernatural uncivilized constitution.

When the caste system is applied incorrectly, which is how it is currently applied around the world, it creates inequality or discrimination, and it is responsible for the red colonization of the world. The misapplication of the caste system creates conditions for demonism to flourish.

The caste system under the political rule of law creates inequality, oppression or domination, lawlessness, poverty, etcetera. The caste system under the legal rule of law eliminates inequality, oppression or domination, poverty, and is used for the purpose of establishing the rule of law. Deviations or variations of the legal caste system are political, the creation of politics, inviting challenges from other political factions that want their political variation to be dominant. This suggests that lies or disobedience created politics or demonism.

The differences between the civil and supernatural

constitutions confirm that insecurities in the economic system, transportation, health, feeding, etcetera are demonic attacks on vulnerable civil beings without supernatural powers and senses from supernatural beings with supernatural powers and senses.

The civil legal constitution, without supernatural powers and senses, is the constitution of a ruler amongst the gods, and the civil being cannot take a break or time off from being a ruler because being a ruler is natural.

It is ridiculous that given the differences between the civil and supernatural beings or the existence of civil and supernatural beings that a supernatural being should be referred to as head of state or the head of a civil legal state rather than a civil legal being.

The uncivilized supernatural being selected or elected as the head of state of a civilization rather than a civil legal being is illogical. This is because the civil scientific being without supernatural powers and senses is the doctrine or legal framework that a civilization is based on.

The custom or tradition of the commoners, supernatural beings, bowing or prostrating to a civil noble being, is a symbolic way of reassuring the civil noble person that they, supernatural beings, will be law abiding, or will behave appropriately given their uncivilized barbaric constitutions.

Author's biography

My name is Lord Loveday Ememe. I was born in the United Kingdom, and of African origin.

I am a graduate of an Anglican seminary school. I graduated from the University of East London with an honours degree in law.

I am of a civil noble constitution.

Bibliography

The Bible

William Shakespeare's the merchant of Venice

The Apartheid regime in South Africa from 1948 to 27 April 1994